· MY · FIRST · LOOK · AT ·

Colours

DK

DORLING KINDERSLEY • LONDON

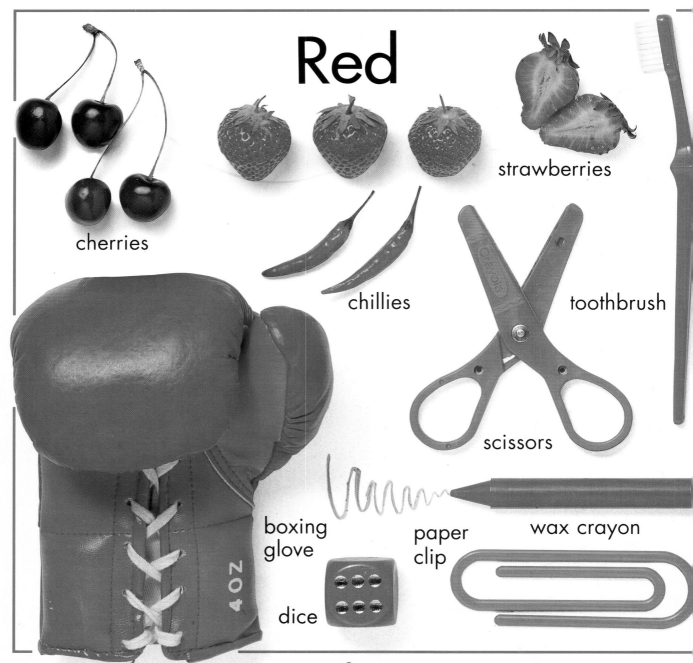

Red

cherries

strawberries

chillies

toothbrush

scissors

boxing glove

paper clip

wax crayon

dice

2

Note to Parents

My First Look at Colours is designed to help young children recognize different colours and learn their names. It's a book for you and your child to share and enjoy - looking at the pages together, finding familiar objects, discovering and comparing their colours, and learning and using new words.

Have fun with colours!

Art Editor Toni Rann
Senior Editor Jane Yorke
Photography Stephen Oliver
Series Consultant Neil Morris
Editorial Director Sue Unstead
Art Director Anne-Marie Bulat

First published in Great Britain in 1990
by Dorling Kindersley Publishers Limited,
9 Henrietta Street, London WC2E 8PS

British Library Cataloguing in Publication Data
My first look at colours
1. Colours
535.6

ISBN 0-86318-424-3

Phototypeset by Windsorgraphics, Ringwood, Hampshire
Reproduced in Hong Kong by Bright Arts
Printed in Italy by L.E.G.O.

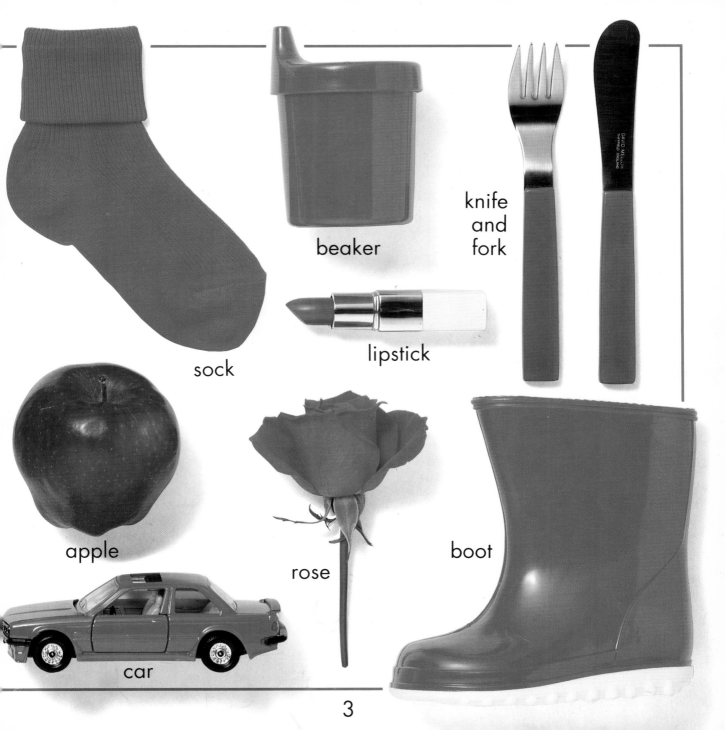

sock

beaker

knife
and
fork

lipstick

apple

rose

boot

car

3

Yellow

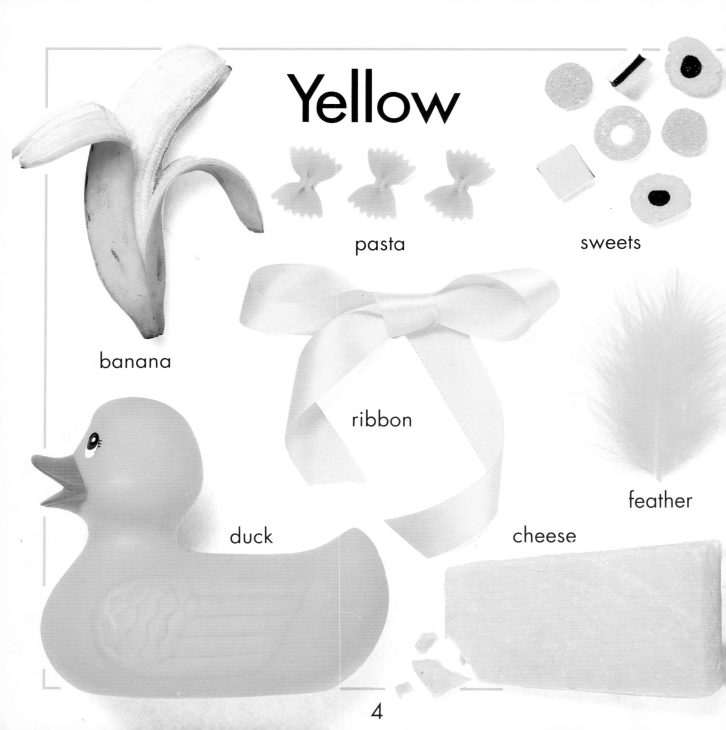

pasta

sweets

banana

ribbon

feather

duck

cheese

4

sponge

lemon

brush

comb

balloon

daffodil

teddy
bear

bricks

5

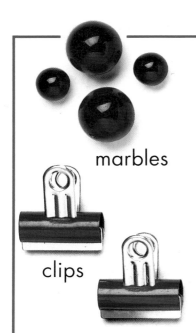

marbles

Blue

bracelet

butterfly

candles

sailor top

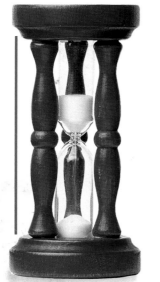

egg-timer

clips

balloon

6

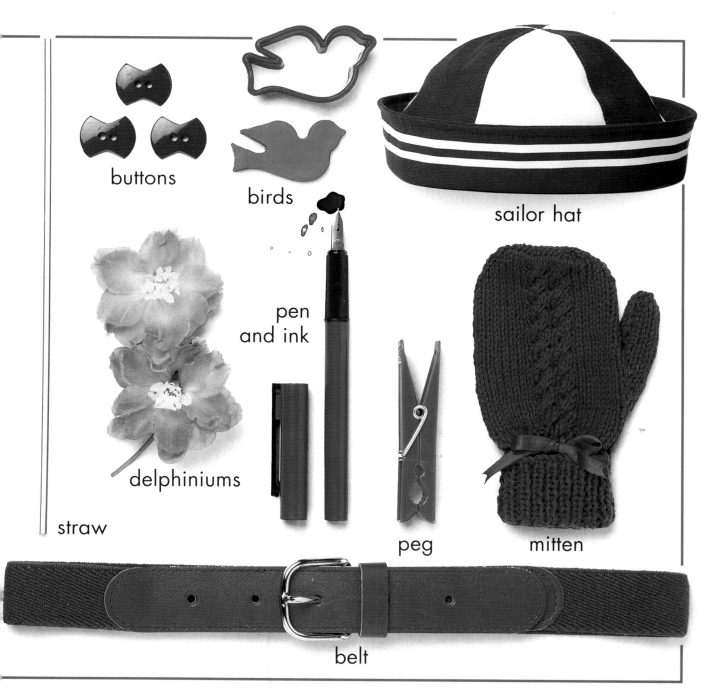

buttons

birds

sailor hat

delphiniums

pen
and ink

straw

peg

mitten

belt

7

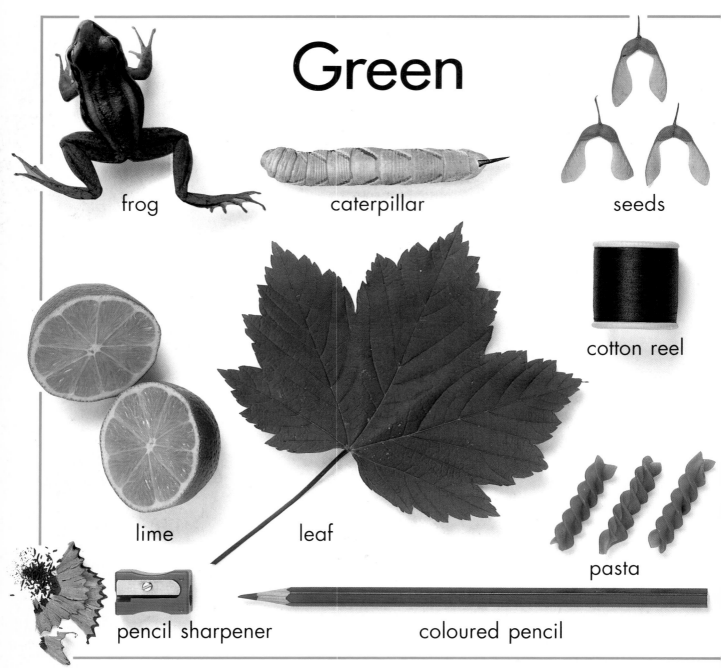

Green

frog

caterpillar

seeds

lime

leaf

cotton reel

pasta

pencil sharpener

coloured pencil

8

pepper

grapes

apple

beans

trees

shells

woolly hat

kiwi
fruit

peas

9

Orange

shell

starfish

carrots

apricot jam

crab

ball

buttons

ice
lolly

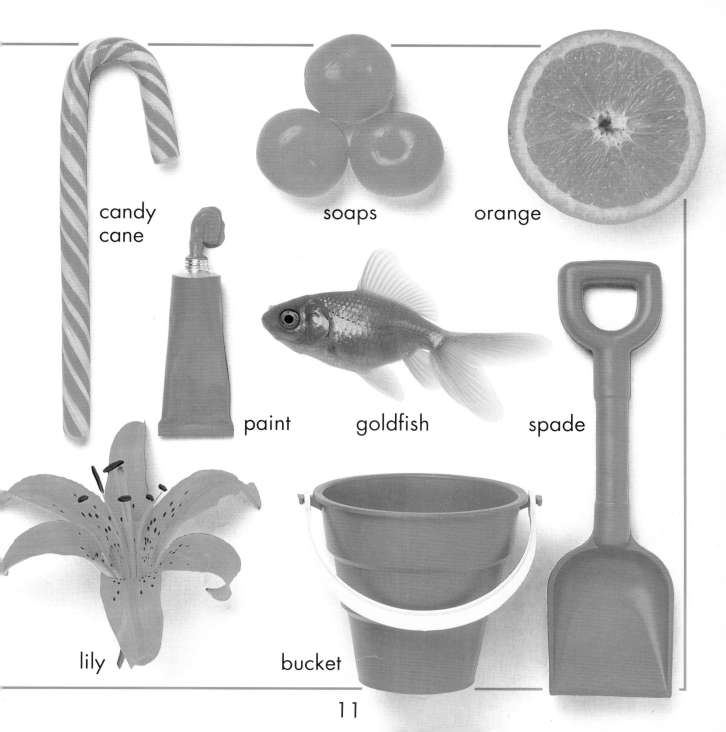

candy
cane

soaps

orange

paint

goldfish

spade

lily

bucket

11

Pink

prawns

coral

beads

safety pins

cake

cotton
wool
balls

soaps

ballet shoes

12

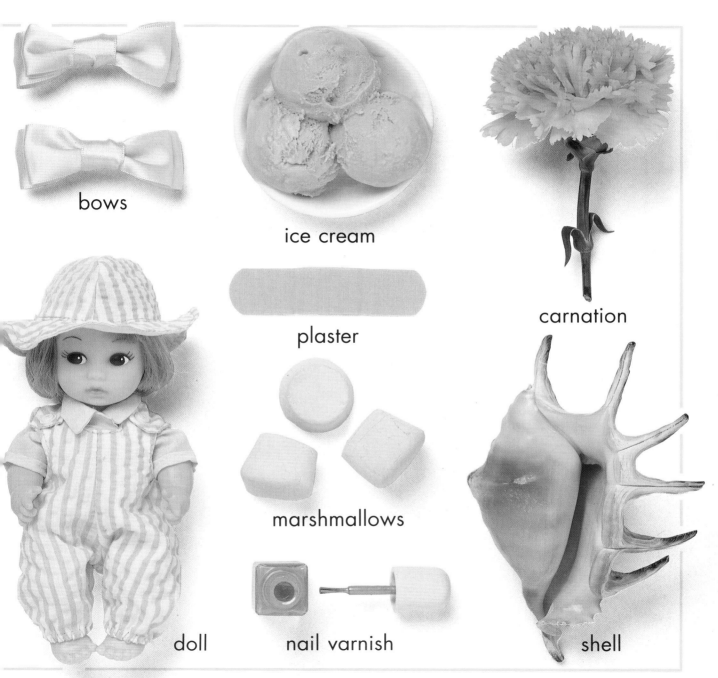

bows

ice cream

carnation

plaster

marshmallows

doll

nail varnish

shell

13

Brown

onions

eggs

leaf

coloured pencils

pine cones

feather

toffees

gingerbread man

bread roll

chocolate ducks

mushrooms

moth

hairbrush

twig

coconut

nuts

brown sugar

Black and white

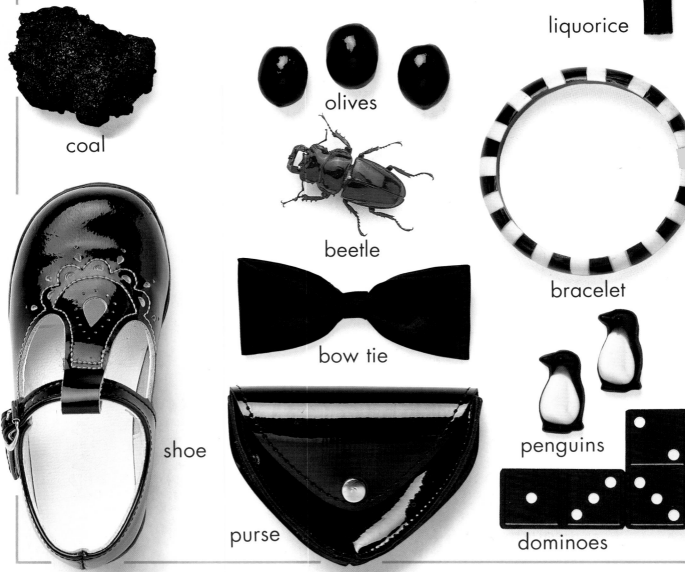

liquorice

coal

olives

beetle

bracelet

shoe

bow tie

purse

penguins

dominoes

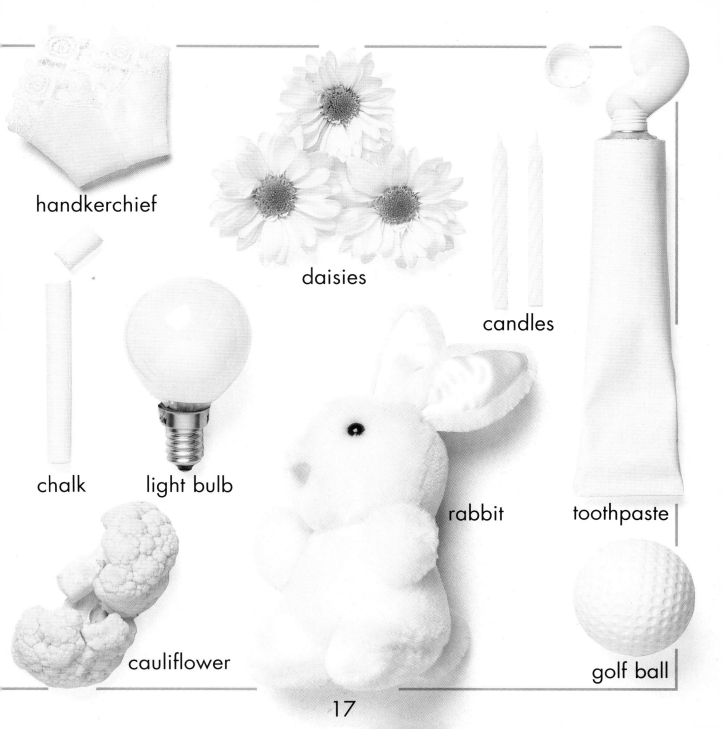

handkerchief

daisies

candles

chalk   light bulb

rabbit   toothpaste

cauliflower

golf ball

17